SCATALOG
A Kid's Field Guide to Animal Poop

HOW TO TRACK A RABBIT

Norman D. Graubart

"BECAUSE EVERYBODY POOPS"

WINDMILL
BOOKS

New York

Published in 2015 by Windmill Books, an Imprint of Rosen Publishing
29 East 21st Street, New York, NY 10010

First Edition

Editor: Katie Kawa
Book Design: Michael J. Flynn

Photo Credits: Cover (rabbit) Guy J. Sagi/Shutterstock.com; cover, pp. 16, 19 (rabbit poop) Emily Veinglory/Shutterstock.com; back cover, pp. 1, 3–12, 14–20, 22–24 (rabbit fur) Ervin Monn/Shutterstock.com; p. 4 Rob Hainer/Shutterstock.com; p. 5 (rabbit) brytta/E+/Getty Images; p. 5 (rabbit poop) wayne marshall/www.flickr.com/photos/wayneandwax/12798078314/CC BY-NC-SA 2.0; p. 6 Dan Bach Kristensen/Shutterstock.com; pp. 7, 8 John P. Ashmore/Shutterstock.com; p. 9 pavalena/Shutterstock.com; p. 10 © iStockphoto.com/lucentius; p. 11 © iStockphoto.com/leekris; p. 12 Kenneth M Highfill/Science Source/Getty Images; p. 13 Jack Milchanowski/Visuals Unlimited/Getty Images; p. 15 (rabbit poop) Emanuele Longo/www.flickr.com/photos/27534429@N08/2700327267/CC BY 2.0; p. 17 Pictoscribe/www.flickr.com/photos/pictoscribe/2512062100/CC BY-NC-ND 2.0; pp. 18, 19 (rabbit tracks) Lars Kastilan/Shutterstock.com; p. 19 (dust bath area) S.J. Krasemann/Photolibrary/Getty Images; p. 19 (rabbit eating) mandritoiu/Shutterstock.com; p. 20 John Kropewnicki/Shutterstock.com; p. 21 Jeff Strickler/Shutterstock.com; p. 22 Michael Chatt/Shutterstock.com.

Library of Congress Cataloging-in-Publication Data

Graubart, Norman D.
How to track a rabbit / by Norman D. Graubart.
p. cm. — (Scatalog: a kid's field guide to animal poop)
Includes index.
ISBN 978-1-4777-5435-1 (pbk.)
ISBN 978-1-4777-5436-8 (6-pack)
ISBN 978-1-4777-5434-4 (library binding)
1. Rabbit — Juvenile literature. 2. Animal droppings — Juvenile literature. I. Graubart, Norman D. II. Title.
QL737.L32 G7318 2015
599.32—d23

Manufactured in the United States of America

CPSIA Compliance Information: Batch # CW15WM: For Further Information contact Rosen Publishing, New York, New York at 1-800-237-9932

CONTENTS

HUNTING RABBITS

Rabbits are very common animals throughout North America. Maybe you've seen one in a park or in your backyard. You might even have one as a pet!

It's not always easy to see rabbits in the wild. They're scared of people and quickly move away when they hear people coming.

Rabbits often leave clues, such as poop and tracks, that hunters can use to find them.

Rabbits are also game for hunters. Hunters find rabbits by tracking them. Hunters track rabbits in different ways. For example, they can follow the footprints rabbits leave on the ground or in the snow. They can also look for fur a rabbit might leave behind. Hunters can even look for rabbit poop to track these animals. Poop tells hunters a lot about rabbits.

COTTONTAILS

There are many **species** of rabbits in North America. There are also animals that look a lot like rabbits, but they have much longer ears. These animals are called hares. Arctic hares live in the coldest parts of North America.

Many people confuse hares and rabbits, but they're not the same animal. Hares such as this one have longer ears, larger bodies, and longer back legs than rabbits.

Arctic hare

6

eastern cottontail

Cottontail rabbits, such as the eastern cottontail shown here, got their name because their tail looks like a ball of cotton!

The most common species of rabbit in North America is the eastern cottontail. Eastern cottontails have fur that can be different shades of brown and gray. They also have a white, fluffy tail. An eastern cottontail is usually about 15 to 18 inches (38 to 46 cm) long and weighs 2 to 3 pounds (0.9 to 1.4 kg).

There are many different species of cottontails. The desert cottontail lives mostly in the southwestern part of the United States. Mountain cottontails live in the Rocky Mountains and Pacific Northwest. Eastern cottontails live mostly in the eastern half of North America, as well as small parts of the Northwest and Southwest.

Rabbits can be a bother in neighborhoods. They eat vegetables out of people's backyard gardens.

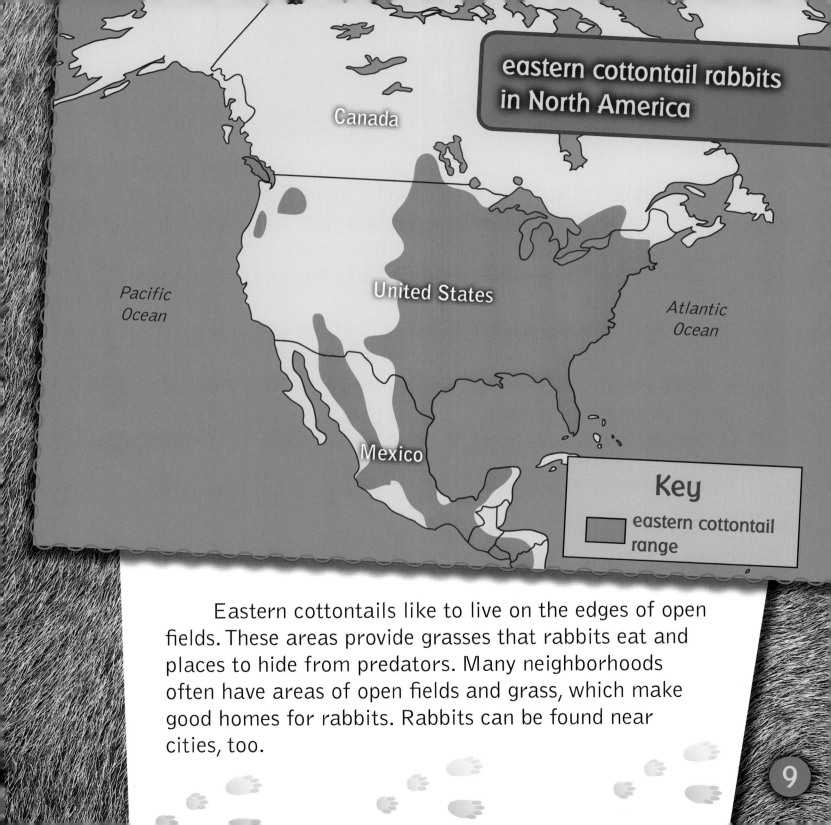

Canada

Pacific
Ocean

United States

Atlantic
Ocean

Mexico

Key

eastern cottontail range

Eastern cottontails like to live on the edges of open fields. These areas provide grasses that rabbits eat and places to hide from predators. Many neighborhoods often have areas of open fields and grass, which make good homes for rabbits. Rabbits can be found near cities, too.

RABBIT RANGES

Rabbits live in an area called a home range. Home ranges are places where rabbits eat, sleep, and **mate**. Male eastern cottontails live on home ranges of up to 100 acres (40.5 ha). Females live on smaller home ranges.

Rabbits spend a lot of the day resting and hiding from predators. They're nocturnal, which means they're most active at night. This is when they look for food.

Finding rabbit poop is a sign that you're in a rabbit's home range.

The size of a rabbit's home range depends on how much food is in an area. If there isn't a lot of food, the size of the home range increases as rabbits travel farther to find food.

Eastern cottontail rabbits spend most of their time alone. They don't live in families or groups. They only spend time with other rabbits during the mating season and when mothers raise baby rabbits.

Rabbits mate several times each year. Mating happens from February to September, depending on where the rabbits live. A female rabbit **protects** her babies in a ground nest on her home range for about a month. After that time, the rabbits live on their own. Rabbits are fully grown after about three months.

Rabbits have been known to live more than 10 years in the wild. However, they don't often live more than a couple of years. Rabbits have many predators, including foxes, owls, and humans.

A litter is a group of baby rabbits born at the same time. Each litter of eastern cottontails commonly has between three and eight babies in it.

Nests for baby rabbits can be found in holes in the ground as well as hollow parts of logs. A hunter who finds a nest knows the mother rabbit is nearby.

EATING POOP!

Rabbits are herbivores. This means they eat plants. During the summer, rabbits eat a lot of grass. They also eat berries and even vegetables from people's gardens. In the winter, rabbits eat woody plant parts, such as twigs and bark.

Rabbits **digest** their food a little differently than most other animals. Some **nutrients** from their food are **absorbed** by body parts called intestines. However, rabbits also have to eat some of their own poop to get the rest of the nutrients they need. Rabbits have two kinds of poop: brown and green. The green kind is the one they eat.

RABBIT DIGESTIVE SYSTEM

A rabbit's cecum is larger than its stomach. Bacteria in the cecum break down plant matter into nutrients the rabbit needs. Rabbits get these nutrients from eating cecal pellets, which is another name for the green poop their body makes.

mouth

intestines

stomach

cecum

After rabbits eat their own cecal pellets, their poop is brown. This is because it's now just the waste left over after everything they've eaten has been digested.

"Pellet" is a general name for a small piece of animal poop. If a hunter sees round or oval-shaped pellets of rabbit poop, a rabbit could be nearby. Green poop in an area means that a rabbit must be close, because rabbits eat their cecal pellets soon after the pellets come out of their body. Hunters commonly only find brown rabbit poop because green poop is eaten so quickly.

Wet rabbit poop is fresh rabbit poop. The rabbit that left it can't be too far away.

There's no noticeable difference between the poop left behind by male rabbits and female rabbits. It's also hard to tell a rabbit's size by looking at the pellets left behind. Most rabbit poop looks the same.

Rabbit pellets can be found in piles near areas where rabbits eat. If a hunter finds a pile of pellets, they know they're in a rabbit's home range.

FOLLOW THE TRACKS!

Hunters also look for rabbit tracks. Hunters often find these tracks in the snow. Rabbits have bigger back feet than front feet, so their tracks show two big prints and two smaller ones. Rabbit tracks also show four toes on each foot. Rabbits jump in a zigzag pattern when they're escaping danger, so hunters look for zigzag tracks.

The smaller front feet of a rabbit touch the ground at different times, which is why the prints aren't next to each other. The larger back feet push off the ground and land at the same time, which is why their prints can be found side by side.

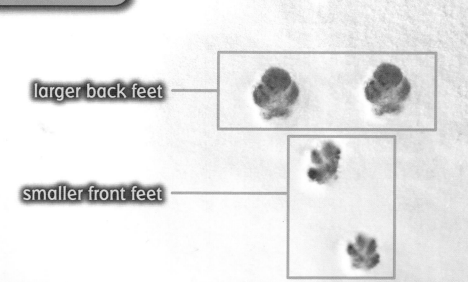

four toes

larger back feet

smaller front feet

RABBIT SIGNS

POOP
- small, round or oval-shaped pellets
- found in groups
- green (rarely found) or brown

TRACKS
- back prints larger than front prints
- large amount of space between tracks because rabbits leap
- four toes on each print

DUST BATH AREA
- areas of sand or dry soil rabbits roll in to get rid of bugs on their body
- about 1 foot (30 cm) wide
- no plants in the area

FEEDING AREAS
- flowering plants have just the stems and no flowers
- angled marks show where rabbits bit the plants
- grass and weeds cut very close to the ground

Hunters look for rabbit feeding areas, too. These have stems, twigs, and flowers that have been partly eaten by a rabbit. Rabbits chew at an angle, so hunters can easily see where they've been eating.

SMELLS AND SOUNDS

Hunters often bring along dogs when they go rabbit hunting. Bloodhounds and beagles have a great sense of smell, which helps them track rabbits.

Cottontail rabbits make certain sounds that also help dogs and hunters find them. When a rabbit is in danger, it screams. However, the sound rabbits are best known for is a thump. They make this sound by tapping their big back feet against the ground. The thumping sound tells other rabbits to look out for predators, such as hunters and their dogs.

Humans can't smell the scent rabbits leave behind, but dogs can. This is why dogs often play a large role in hunting rabbits.

If a hunter hears a thumping sound, they know a rabbit must be close.

21

RABBITS IN THE WILD

Rabbits are cute animals, but they can take over a neighborhood. Rabbit hunting helps control the number of rabbits in an area. There are millions of rabbits in North America. This means people can hunt them without upsetting the **ecosystem**.

Wild rabbits, such as eastern cottontails, are different from the rabbits kept as pets. If you have a pet rabbit, don't try to send it into the wild. It won't survive. Both pet rabbits and wild rabbits are fun to learn about and watch.

GLOSSARY

absorb (uhb-ZOHRB) To take in or soak up.

digest (dy-JEHST) To break down food into something the body can use.

ecosystem (EE-koh-sihs-tuhm) A community of living things.

mate (MAYT) To come together to make babies.

nutrient (NOO-tree-uhnt) Something taken in by a plant or animal that helps it grow and stay healthy.

protect (pruh-TEHKT) To keep safe.

species (SPEE-sheez) A group of living things that are all the same kind.

INDEX

WEBSITES

For web resources related to the subject of this book, go to:
www.windmillbooks.com/weblinks and select this book's title.